AUSTRALIA

A PICTURE BOOK TO REMEMBER HER BY

Designed by
DAVID GIBBON

Produced by
TED SMART

CRESCENT

INTRODUCTION

The great English explorer Captain Cook, during his voyage of discovery in the 18th century, first sighted the coastline of Australia from his ship 'Endeavour'. He could hardly have imagined, at the time, the enormous size of the land mass he had chanced upon – a great new continent of nearly three million square miles of astonishingly diverse countryside that amazes the first-time visitor even today.

Settlers originally came from England and later from all over the world, leaving their homelands for the challenge of a new life in an undeveloped country. In these 200 years of settlement, the population has gradually increased to its present total of 14 million. The people now share a single language and live happily alongside the Aboriginals in the warm and sunny climate of the continent.

Australia is divided into six states and one territory. New South Wales and Victoria, both on the eastern seaboard, have by far the largest populations. The state of Western Australia is the biggest, containing within its boundaries the Great Sandy, Gibson and Great Victoria deserts. Darwin is the capital of the Northern Territory, and the other states are South Australia, Queensland and the island of Tasmania.

Although Canberra is the capital of Australia, Sydney is its largest city. It is also the busiest seaport, and Australia's commercial centre, with many modern Skyscrapers standing proudly against the skyline. It was to this area that the first settlers came in the 1780's, and it has grown in importance ever since.

Sydney is universally renowned for its bridge across the picturesque natural harbour, and an abundance of sailing boats tacking back and forth across its waters is indicative of the Australian's love of sport, and, indeed, of all outdoor activities. Nearby are many beautiful beaches and the lucky residents of Sydney can take advantage of these at the weekends to improve their golden sun-tans, whilst watching the expert surfers speed by, riding the white-crested waves. A family day out on the beach with a picnic basket and a few ice-cold beers is a typical Sunday for the fortunate people who live near this magnificent coastline.

Sydney is also a great cultural centre and many of the fine singers, dancers, musicians and artists who studied at its various academies have become internationally acclaimed and have thrilled audiences throughout the world.

Melbourne, the second largest city in Australia with a population of 2.75 million, is the capital of Victoria and boasts a "garden atmosphere" of tree-lined avenues and beautiful parks. One particular feature of the city is the famous old trams which still run along the bustling streets. Melbourne has a very enthusiastic sporting public and its famous cricket ground, which has a capacity of over 125,000, has staged the 1956 Olympic Games, many international cricket matches and is also the home of Australian Rules Football. Every year in November the running of the Melbourne Cup, a century-old horse race, takes place in beautiful surroundings, drawing very large crowds as it is considered a fashionable social event. Outside the city of Melbourne the countryside is green and fertile, and is a natural wildlife and bird sanctuary.

The Great Barrier Reef of Australia is considered to be one of nature's masterpieces. It runs parallel to the coast along the north-eastern shore of Queensland and is a marine enthusiast's paradise. This chain of small coral islands provides a unique opportunity for underwater study, being inhabited by thousands of different species of sea creatures. The waters along the reef are so free from pollution that it is possible to have a remarkably clear view of the underwater life. The reef is also a favourite fishing area where game fish abound, and trips by boat around these islands to try one's luck at catching marlin are in great demand.

Farming was the original industry of Australia and it still plays an extremely important part in her world trade. Thousands of square miles covered by sheep and cattle farms, called "stations" provide an agricultural area vaster than anywhere else in the world. A large percentage of the world's wool is produced and exported from Australia, and their excellent meat and dairy produce is also sent overseas. Fruit farms and vineyards abound, especially in the Murray River and Barossa Valley districts, and Australian wines are enjoyed abroad as well as in their own country. Farmers can grow a variety of vegetables and also plant corn, sugar cane, cotton and trees, for Australia also has an important timber industry.

Captain Charles Sturt headed the first expedition into the centre of Australia from Adelaide in 1844. He is quoted as having declared it: "a landscape which never changes but for the worse", and turned back! In comparison with the rest of Australia these regions still look empty on the map, and it was years before men determined to travel to and then settle in what has now become known as the "Red Centre". The area still offers a harsh existence to its inhabitants due to the great droughts and the high temperature which often soars over 100 degrees.

This area presents the image that many people hold of the "real" Australia: land of the bushman and drover with the Aborigines hunting with spears against the dramatic background of nature's landmarks – a life we think of as a true pioneer existence.

Alice Springs, in the heart of Australia, was once a typical central town with simple corrugated-iron roofed houses and bars which were used by parched travellers on their journeys through the continent. Now modern hotels have been built from which the nearby ranges can be explored and photographed, and the bright wild flowers which, if blessed by a shower of rain, quickly come into bloom and transform the area into one of outstanding natural beauty.

The great golden orb of the sun sinks into the sea *left*
at Darwin in the Northern Territory.

Brisbane seen in the magnificent aerial view *left,* the capital and chief port of Queensland, is situated on Moreton Bay near the mouth of the Brisbane River.

The hard steel of Story Bridge *bottom right* is transformed into delicate filigree against the glow of the setting sun, and *right* sodium lighting casts an eerie light across Captain Cook Bridge.

Named after Sir Thomas Brisbane, the then Governor of New South Wales, Brisbane was originally a penal colony and became a free settlement in 1842. Today it is a well-planned modern city, with fine parks and streets and many attractive buildings *above and centre right.*

The leisure activities within Moreton Bay are particularly splendid and include game fishing grounds, ocean-side golf courses and the ever-popular race courses.

The vast metropolis of Brisbane, fringed by a belt of green, sprawls along the banks of the river *overleaf.*

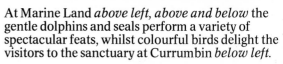

At Marine Land *above left, above and below* the gentle dolphins and seals perform a variety of spectacular feats, whilst colourful birds delight the visitors to the sanctuary at Currumbin *below left*.

Queensland is Australia's second largest state and its tropical climate is ideally suited to many water-sports, such as sailing *right* where colourful, billowing spinnakers stretch against the wind and *below* a surfer rides high on the crest of a wave.

The sailing vessel *bottom right* is typical of those used in deep-sea waters for a catch of marlin and shark.

Golf *below* on Dunk Island, is an ever-popular sport as is local racing *centre right,* the horses thundering along a red, dirt track.

Wide, sandy beaches stretching along Queensland's Pacific Coast *left and centre left* are a constant attraction to Australia's sun-loving citizens.

The huge waves and frothing spume *right, below right and below* provide an exciting playground for those with nerves of steel who enjoy the thrill of surfing as the crashing breakers roll and thunder above their heads.

Although the sea offers much enjoyment, its vastness makes it necessary to have a well disciplined team of lifeguards *left and below* constantly on hand and ever-alert to the possible danger of any calamities.

Sugar cane *top left* and tobacco *far left* thrive in Queensland's hot and humid climate.

At Atherton, in the north, lush rain forests *left,* tumbling waterfalls and serene crater lakes are typical of the scenery.

Queensland, with its large open plains, is the chief state for beef-raising and vast herds of cattle and stockmen are a common sight as *above,* where the drover drives the cattle along the dusty track.

In the more temperate and fertile south sheep are grazed; the most important breed being the thick-coated merino *right.*

The Great Barrier Reef, the world's longest chain of coral reefs, is an important resort area noted for its sunshine, spectacular marine life and the world's largest oysters. Swooping low over the sandy shoreland can be seen huge flocks of birds *left*.

In the Lone Pine Sanctuary *below* the lovable koalas thrive, feeding almost entirely on eucalyptus shoots.

Off the coast, near Cairns, unusual fish like Red Emperor, Scarlet Perch and Coral Trout are caught with the aid of the well-equipped game fishing boats *below left*.

Fishing boats and pleasure craft fill the lovely harbour at Townsville *centre left*, Queensland's second largest city.

Soft clouds blow over Coolangatta *below* which is a popular resort situated on Brisbane's 'Gold Coast'.

In a silver sea at Nelson *right* the pretty yachts glide gracefully, in this favourite yachting centre.

Sydney *top left and centre left,* Australia's largest city and the capital of New South Wales, lies on Port Jackson, four miles west of the Pacific Ocean. It is also the country's oldest city and today, a cosmopolitan centre with international hotels, restaurants and nightclubs.

The revolutionary, multi-shelled Sydney Opera House *right* was opened in 1973 and is surrounded on three sides by the waters of the harbour.

Sydney Harbour Bridge seen in the magnificent aerial views *above and far left,* was completed in 1932 and connects the northern, residential side of the harbour with the industrial side to the south.

The metropolitan area with its twisting highways *left* now extends as far south as Botany Bay.

The S.S. Canberra, glimmering in an eerie light, can be seen *centre left* in the floodlit glow of the harbour bridge, and the exciting night spot of Luna Park with its dazzling illuminations is shown *bottom left.*

Sydney's imposing Town Hall is pictured *left* and *below* the colourful fireworks display lights up the city shoreline.

Undulatory waves lap the superb surfing beach of Manly *right,* which is just one of the many to be found both to the north and south of Sydney.

The full white sails of the gleaming craft *below* take advantage of the gentle breeze as it blows across Sydney Harbour.

Sydney's miles of golden beaches and clear blue waters are a constant pleasure to the hard working Australians who enjoy their leisure hours to the full.

North of Sydney is Whale Beach *right*, Manly Beach *centre left* and Bungar Beach *bottom left*.

Fabulous Bondi Beach *below right*, Sydney's most famous recreation area, lies to the south of the city, as does Coogie Beach *left*.

With miles of pounding breakers and flying foam *above* it is not surprising that Australia produces a large number of surfing champions, as the opportunities for constant practice are obviously numerous.

Golfing, at the New South Wales Golf Course *below*, is an ever-popular sport and particularly pleasurable when, as here, the greens are smooth and velvety.

New South Wales is the leading pastoral and agricultural state and cattle-raising *right* is of prime importance.

The wide, open spaces at Hunter Valley *left* and Mudgee *below,* are ideal for cattle farming and also for sheep-rearing, shown at San Michele *below right.*

Santa Gertrudis bulls can be seen grazing in the tranquil Milton Park, Bowral *left.*

Australian wine has a fine reputation and *below left* is the lovely Lindermans Ben Ean Vineyard at Pokolbin, Hunter Valley, nestling in the lee of the misty mountains.

With brede of patchwork the central channelled bands of green on green in the Darling Downs *below,* resemble the brushwork of a contemporary artist.

The Sydney-Newcastle Expressway *right* snakes through the magnificent and densely packed greenery of some of the beautiful national parks situated in New South Wales.

Surrounded by a sea of red dust, Broken Hill *above* is often called the Silver City because of its huge silver mines, which are the largest in the world.

The grime and smoke of the industrial area of Port Kembla *left* is sharply contrasted with the clear blue ocean in the background.

The peaceful scene *left* is of the fishing fleet at Ulladulla and *below* can be seen the gum trees which are an integral part of the Australian landscape.

The softly shimmering reflections on Tuggerah Lake provide a delightful setting for the resting pelicans *centre left*.

Old Sydney Town *above right* is a reconstructed replica of Sydney Cove and is sited seventy km. north of Sydney. The Cove was originally an early settlement, founded in 1788, from which the city of Sydney later developed.

The fascinating historical museum at Cooma is well worth a visit. The remodelled farm kitchen interior *right* illustrates the austerity of the lives of the early settlers.

The well-landscaped federal capital of
Canberra, situated on a tributary of the
Murrumbidgee River, can be seen in the
superb aerial views *above, top left and
far left.* Planned by W. B. Griffin, a
Chicago architect, the foundation stone
was laid in 1913. Although the
Commonwealth Parliament was
originally based in Melbourne, the
authority was transferred to Canberra
in 1927 and since that time the city has
rapidly expanded.

The magnificent, floodlit Parliament
House is shown *centre left,* and *right*
the impressive Memorial and shooting
jet of water in the blue bay is a fitting
tribute to the British explorer Captain
Cook.

Pictured *left* is the space tracking
station at Tidbinbilla.

Melbourne, the capital of Victoria, is the second city of Australia and its development accelerated in 1851, after the gold rush.

Today the city has many lovely parks as well as botanical and zoological gardens and amongst its most notable buildings are the Anglican and Roman Catholic Cathedrals.
The city's modern skyline *right* is reflected in a shimmering green glow along the water's edge.

Most of Melbourne's industries are situated in the city and include oil refining, meat processing and engineering. This busy sea-port includes Williamstown and handles a large portion of the Commonwealth shipping.

Sunlight glints on the skyscrapers *right* lining the Yarra River.

Attractive Colliers Street, with its old trams, is shown *left*, and *centre right* is the busy Royal Arcade.

The white turrets of the splendid Exhibition Building, bordered by lush green trees, are serenely mirrored in the blue waters of the lake *above*.

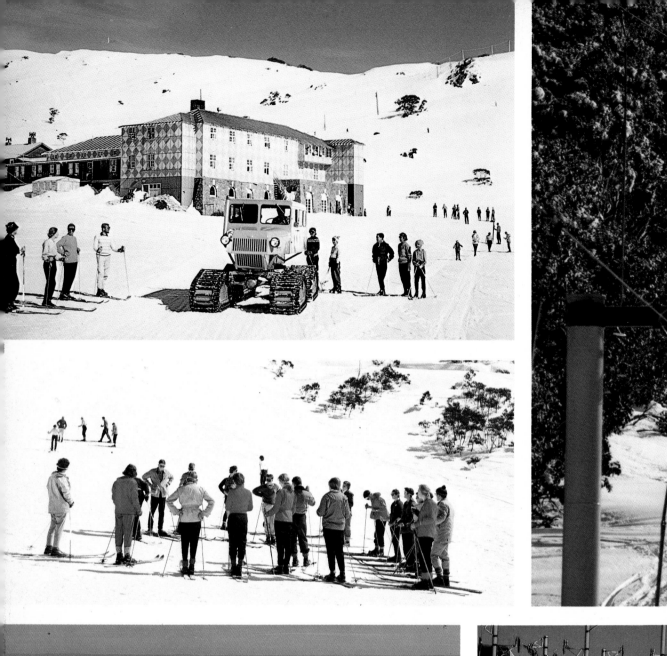

Although the Snowy Mountains are
part of the Australian Alps, they are, in
fact, a series of tableland and the
magnificent Mt Kosciusko *top left* is
the highest peak at 2,230m.

The Snowy Mountains hydroelectric
scheme conserves the torrents of water
which flow in the Springtime thaw after
the thickly encrusted snow-capped
winter months. The Talbingo Dam,
completed in 1970, is the largest dam in
the scheme.

Skiing facilities are excellent *centre left*
and can rival any to be found in the rest
of the world.

Another popular ski-resort area is
Mount Buller *above, left and far left*,
lying south-west of the mountains.

At Mount Hotham *right* a helicopter
serves as an unusual ski-lift.

Australia offers many sporting facilities and at Sandringham, Victoria *left*, the pretty yachts bob in a sea of glistening waves.

Cricket at Melbourne Club *centre left*, and racing, particularly the Melbourne Cup *bottom left*, held each November, are also popular sports.

Sovereign Hill Historical Park *right* is an interesting tourist attraction, with its 'Puffing Billy' steam train *below right*, which wends its way through wooded hills and fern gullies in the Dandenong Mountains.

Horse riding *above* is an enjoyable way of seeing the more remote parts of Victoria.

Every March, in Melbourne, is held a Moomba Festival *below* with an exotic dragon parade.

Along sections of Victoria's coastline can be seen spectacular examples of natural arches and stacks.

At Port Campbell *bottom left,* in a beautiful azure sea, stand a group of stacks also shown *below* and aptly named 'The Apostles'.

Inland the scenery is equally awe-inspiring, particularly in the region of the Granpians *left,* where from the 'Devil's Jaw', two climbers look out across the remote and hilly scrubland.

'London Bridge' *centre left* is a natural stone formation washed by blue-green waters and tinged with a russet hue in the afternoon sunshine.

Darkly dramatic, the 'Grotto' *right* at Ocean Road lends a sinister air to this dramatic spot, from where the gentle blue sea merges into a soft grey horizon.

The kangaroo *right and above* is possibly the most famous of Australia's indigenous animals. Although only one inch long at birth it quickly attains its full-grown height of approximately 8ft. With well-developed hind legs and a strong tail, these marsupials can travel at speed in long leaps.

With the exception of the ostrich, the emu *left*, is the largest of living birds and found only in Australia. The pouch in the female's windpipe enables it to emit the characteristic, loud and booming note.

The sweet-faced koala bears *overleaf* are difficult to rear in zoos because of their dependence on eucalyptus shoots in their diet. For many years they were hunted for their fur and were practically exterminated. However, for the past forty years, they have been a protected species and their numbers, in consequence, have been greatly restored.

Tasmania is a small island off the south coast of the mainland. Much of the island is mountainous and there are numerous lakes and rivers that have been harnessed to provide electricity.

The incredible caves with massive stalactites and stalagmites *above* are a feature of the Cave Reserves within the island.

Hobart, the capital, *left* is situated on the estuary of the Derwent River and has a fine harbour, and *below and above right* can be seen the city's splendid Constitution Dock.

The soft diffusion of a golden sunrise over Sandy Bay is pictured *right*, the sky heavy with drifting birds.

Launceston, a prosperous commercial centre trading with the mainland, was founded in 1805 and amongst its manufacturing industries is the important woollen trade. The photograph *left* shows an unusual street of churches with contrasting architectural designs.

The impressive Tasman Bridge *right* provides a vital link as it snakes across the dark blue waters of the Derwent River. The river itself supplies power to several hydroelectric stations and flows to a wide estuary on Storm Bay.

Picturesque Wrest Point, Hobart, with pretty white houses nestling along the banks of the beautiful bay is shown *above*, with its impressive casino dominating the foreground. This was the first licensed casino to be built on Australian soil.

Named after the queen of William IV, and founded in 1836, Adelaide, the capital of South Australia, stands on high ground overlooking Holdfast Bay.

The impressive aerial view *above left* shows a noteworthy example of town planning and the city has many impressive streets like Victoria Square *left*, and King William Street *far left*.

The attractive North Adelaide Public Golf Course can be seen *right*.

One of Adelaide's major festivals is the Highland Games *above right*, with the pipers clad in traditional Scottish dress.

South Australia has the largest wine producing area in the country and a climate, along the coast, comparable to that of the Mediterranean.

Most of the picturesque vineyards are in the Barossa Valley *right* and were first planted by German settlers in 1847. Every other year their descendants hold a two-day Vintage Festival *above right*.

The meticulously laid out citrus groves in a dark green landscape can be seen *left*.

Part of the long, dusty Sturt Highway from Adelaide to New South Wales is shown *centre left*, and *top left* the beautiful scenery in the Mount Gambier area.

Animals like the koala bear *far right* can be seen at close quarters in the Cleland National Park.

Western Australia, the largest state, covers more than a third of the continent. Its capital, Perth, is the sunshine city, where over 6,000 varieties of flowers and blooming plants, unique to Australia, can be seen.

The pictures *left and right* show many of Perth's skyscrapers but the city also has some fine old buildings.

London Court *above left and above* is a quaint Tudor-style arcade of small shops adjoining the main shopping centre, whilst *below* is Winthrop Hall, one of Perth's delightful university buildings.

The splendid, floodlit Parliament House can be seen *below left*.

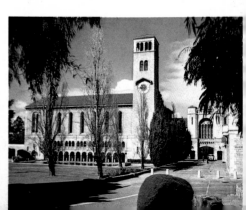

Modern lighting casts a red glow over the old stalactites and stalagmites in the limestone caves *top left* near Margaret River.

The breathtaking Dales Gorge *far left* is in the Hamersley Range of mountains.

The Indian Ocean is rich in shellfish and pearls and the offshore pearl lugger *left* plies the tranquil sea searching for these highly prized gems.

In the tropical north the channelled rice fields *above* are set like dominoes and shown *right* is a typical western Australian sunset, with scurrying clouds in an amber sky.

The Aborigines, the native people of Australia, live a fascinating existence with customs that have changed little over the years.

Collecting shellfish *left* off Groote Island, Northern Territory, are some Aboriginal women with their children and *below* an artist from Elcho Island proudly displays his work.

Kangaroo meat is an essential part of the Aborigines' diet and the photograph *below left* shows the meat as it is being prepared for cooking.

Turtle eggs are also eaten and the collection *below* was photographed on Wessell Island.

Aborigines from Western Australia are shown *above right* in ceremonial dress, carrying their all-important spears, whilst *below* is an Aboriginal camp at Caledon Bay.

Australia's great outback, in the heart of the country, has been named the 'Red Centre' because of the huge stretches of red-sand desert *above* and vast mountain ranges *left*. Roads are few and lakes and rivers dry up in this parched land.

South of Alice Springs can be seen the famous Aboriginal rock carvings at Ooraminna which are thought to be between 6,000 and 10,000 years old.

Many Aborigines now work on sheep stations, cattle ranches and also in the rich Australian mines.

Banana Plantations also provide employment for the native Aborigines, such as the happy-looking worker seen *right* on Elcho Island, which lies off the coast of the Northern Territory, in the Arafura Sea.

Spectacular colour changes at sunrise and sunset highlight Ayers Rock *above and left* which attains this incredible distinction by reflecting and absorbing the rays of the sun.

Standing 335m high, the rock is 9 kilometres round and is the world's largest monolith.

Such a popular tourist attraction is this region that there is no shortage of visitors *below*, anxious to enjoy one of the 'outback tours'.

A desolate, wind carved rock face, typical of those in Australia's interior can be seen *right*.

Alice Springs *below* is a green oasis in the middle of Australia. Originally a telegraph station, it is now a tourist centre, headquarters of the flying doctor service and an important opal mining town.

The camels *left*, with their ability to travel long distances without water, make extremely useful desert companions.

An aerial view of a cattle station and homestead *left*, bordered by a billabong, typifies the isolated conditions in which many farmers live.

Stark mountain ranges and stretches of red-sand desert are a familiar sight in the Great Outback *below*.

Darwin *right*, the capital of Northern Territory, was named after Charles Darwin. Devastated by a typhoon, the city is now in the process of being rebuilt.

A 1,600 Km. bitumen highway *above right* links Darwin with the town of Alice Springs.

The majestic but uninhabitable Macdonnel Ranges are shown *left and above*, near Alice Springs in Northern Territory.

Also in Northern Territory is Elcho Island, just off the coast at Arnhem Land and pictured *right* is an Aborigine standing on a wind-sculptured peak at Sacred Rocks.

Cattle drovers can be seen *below* in the desert land surrounding Alice Springs.

The hot arid desert of Simpson, in Northern Territory *overleaf*, is sharply contrasted with the moody clouds lowering in the sky above.

First published in Great Britain 1978 by Colour Library International Ltd.
© Illustrations: Colour Library International Ltd. Colour separations by La Cromolito, Milan, Italy.
Display and text filmsetting by Focus Photoset, London, England.
Printed and bound by SAGDOS - Brugherio (MI), Italy.
Published by Crescent Books, a division of Crown Publishers Inc.
Library of Congress Catalogue Card No. 77-18461
CRESCENT 1978